Spelling

Pupil Book **Year 2**

Shelley Welsh

Features of this book

- Clear explanations and worked examples for spelling topics from the KS1 National Curriculum.

- Questions split into three sections that become progressively more challenging:

Warm up

Test yourself

Challenge yourself

- 'How did you do?' checks at the end of each topic for self-evaluation.

- Regular progress tests to assess pupils' understanding and recap on their learning.

- Answers to every question in a pull-out section at the centre of the book.

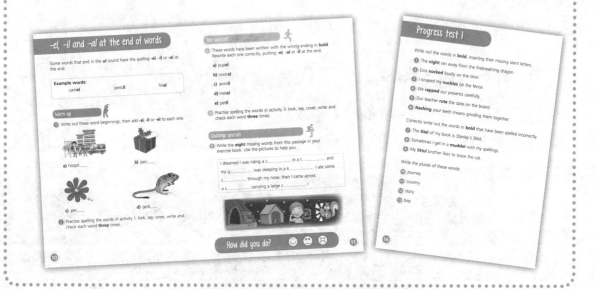

Contents

Silent k and g at the beginning of words

Words that start with **k** or **g** followed by the letter **n** are pronounced with just the **n** sound.

But hundreds of years ago, **k** and **g** would have been pronounced as well. Imagine if we pronounced the **k** in **know**: **k-now**.

Example words:

knight	**kn**it	**kn**ob
gnome	**gn**aw	**gn**ash

Warm up

1. Copy the words in the columns. Then match the incorrectly spelled words on the left to the correct spellings on the right. One has been done for you.

   a) nome   knuckle

   b) nee   gnome

   c) nock   knee

   d) nuckle   knock

2. Practise spelling the words in activity 1: look, say, cover, write and check each word **three** times.

3 Write the word that describes each picture below.

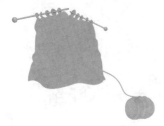

a) ____ife

b) ____aw

c) ____itting

d) ____ash

4 Practise spelling each word from activity 3.
Say the sounds as you write.

5 Write out the missing words in this short passage, using the pictures to help you.

The brave princess saved the scared _____ who was

tied up in the tower. She undid the _____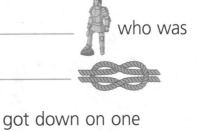

in the rope, then the _____ got down on one

_____ and asked the princess to marry him.

How did you do?

Silent w in wr at the beginning of words

Words that start with **w** followed by **r** are pronounced with just the **r** sound. Say the word *wrap* out loud, then write it in the air using your finger. Remember to pronounce **wr** as *r*!

Example words:

wrap   **wr**ite   **wr**iggle   **wr**ote

Warm up

1. The following words start with **wr** but the letters have been jumbled up! Write them out correctly.

   a) nowrg

   b) twroe

   c) rigglew

   d) parwrep

   e) rstlewe

   f) parw

   g) lekinwr

   h) renw

2 Write out the word beginning with **wr** that is missing in each sentence. Use the pictures to help you.

a) I hurt my _____ playing tennis.

b) My teacher had to _____ a bandage round it.

c) Mum _____ a letter to thank him.

Challenge yourself

3 All of these words start with the **r** sound – but **three** of them have been spelled incorrectly. They should have a letter **w** before the letter **r**, but the **w** is missing. Can you spot which ones they are? Write the correct spellings.

a) reck

b) rip

c) ritten

d) rinkle

e) rope

How did you do?

-le at the end of words

Most words that end in an **ul** sound have the spelling **-le** at the end.

Example words:

tab**le**	app**le**	bott**le**	litt**le**
pudd**le**	cand**le**	wigg**le**	mudd**le**

Say each word in turn out loud, then write it in the air with your finger.

Warm up

① Write out these word beginnings, then add **-le** to each one.

a) ank____

b) jugg____

c) need____

d) pudd____

e) mudd____

f) fidd____

g) hudd____

h) strugg____

② Practise spelling the words in activity 1: look, say, cover, write and check each word **three** times.

3 These words should end with **-le** but have been spelled incorrectly. Write each one correctly **three** times: look, say, cover, write and check.

a) middul

b) cuddul

c) riddul

d) paddul

Challenge yourself

4 Write out the words ending in **-le** that say what each picture is.

a)

b)

c)

d)

-el, -il and -al at the end of words

Some words that end in the **ul** sound have the spelling **-el**, **-il** or **-al** at the end.

> **Example words:**
>
> cam**el**   pen**cil**   fin**al**

1 Write out these word beginnings, then add **-al**, **-il** or **-el** to each one.

a) hospit____

b) parc____

c) pet____

d) gerb____

2 Practise spelling the words in activity 1: look, say, cover, write and check each word **three** times.

3 These words have been written with the wrong ending in **bold**.
Rewrite each one correctly, putting **-el**, **-al** or **-il** at the end.

a) pup**el**

b) nostr**al**

c) anim**il**

d) met**el**

e) pet**il**

4 Practise spelling the words in activity 3: look, say, cover, write and
check each word **three** times.

Challenge yourself

5 Write the **eight** missing words from this passage in your
exercise book. Use the pictures to help you.

I dreamed I was riding a c_____ in a t_____ and

my g_____ was sleeping in a k_____. I ate some

c_____ through my nose, then I came across

a s_____ carrying a large c_____!

How did you do?

11

Adding –s and –es to nouns and verbs ending in *y*

Singular means one of something and **plural** means more than one. For most **nouns**, you just add **-s** to make the **plural**.

But to make the **plural** of **nouns** ending in a consonant plus **y**, you need to change the **y** to **i** then add **-es**.

> **Example nouns:**
>
> baby → babies   lorry → lorries   butterfly → butterflies

Remember! To make the plural of nouns ending in a vowel plus **y** (that's **-ay**, **-ey**, **-oy** or **-uy**), you just add **-s**.

> **Examples:**
>
> monkey → monkeys   boy → boys
>
> tray → trays   guy → guys

When you want to add an **s** to **verbs** (doing or being words) that end in **y**, you follow exactly the same rules.

> **Examples:**
>
> they fly → she flies   you carry → she carries   we cry → he cries
>
> **But:**   I say → she says   you buy → he buys

Warm up

1. Change these nouns from singular to plural.

   a) lady   **b)** country

   c) body   **d)** story

2. Practise spelling the plural nouns in activity 1 **three** times.

3 Copy the table below. Sort the nouns in the box into two groups: those that end in a consonant plus **y** and those that end in a vowel plus **y**. Write the plural forms in the correct places in the table.

key   copy   toy   journey   party   diary   day   city

consonant plus y	vowel plus y

4 Change the verbs in brackets so that they make sense in each sentence. Remember the spelling rules!

a) Dad (hurry) _____ to make the breakfast while Erin (play) _____ games with her brother.

b) Ben (try) _____ hard to learn his spellings, but he (say) _____ they are really hard.

c) The hen (lay) _____ eggs every day, then the farmer (carry) _____ them into the kitchen.

How did you do?

Compound words

A **compound word** is made by combining two words to make one word.

Examples:

bed + time = bedtime

arm + chair = armchair

wind + mill = windmill

butter + cup = buttercup

class + room = classroom

Warm up

1. These compound words have become separated. Put them back together again and write them out. One has been done for you.

a) bed   brush

b) farm   cut

c) dish   print

d) tooth   room

e) foot   yard

f) hair   washer

2 **Four** of these words are compound words. Work out which ones they are, and write them out.

a) butterfly

b) computer

c) eyebrow

d) fireplace

e) window

f) downstairs

3 Add another word to each of these words to make a compound word. You might think of more than one! Write out your words.

a) home

b) play

c) head

d) rain

e) snow

How did you do?

Write out the words in **bold**, inserting their missing silent letters.

1 The **night** ran away from the firebreathing dragon.

2 Ezra **nocked** loudly on the door.

3 I scraped my **nuckles** on the fence.

4 We **rapped** our presents carefully.

5 Our teacher **rote** the date on the board.

6 **Nashing** your teeth means grinding them together.

Correctly write out the words in **bold** that have been spelled incorrectly.

7 The **titel** of my book is *Stanley's Stick*.

8 Sometimes I get in a **muddel** with my spellings.

9 My **littul** brother likes to tease the cat.

Write the plurals of these words:

10 journey

11 country

12 story

13 boy

Complete these words with the correct spelling of the **ul** sound – **-el**, **-il** or **-al**.

14 pet____

15 cam____

16 penc____

The second part of each of these compound words in **bold** is attached to the wrong beginning. Move the second parts around to create four compound words that make sense.

17 light**side**

18 sea**house**

19 under**bin**

20 dust**pants**

Adding suffixes 1

If a word with **one syllable** ends in a single vowel plus a single consonant, you double the consonant before adding the suffixes **-ed**, **-ing**, **-er**, **-est** and **-y**.

Examples:

drop → dro**pp**ed   pa**t** → pa**tt**ed

pa**t** → pa**tt**ing   si**t** → si**tt**ing

fa**t** → fa**tt**er   di**p** → di**pp**er

sa**d** → sa**dd**est   fa**t** → fa**tt**est

su**n** → su**nn**y   ru**n** → ru**nn**y

But watch out! The letter **x** is never doubled.

Examples:

mi**x** → mi**x**ed   bo**x** → bo**x**er

Warm up

1 Add **-ing** to the following words. Remember the spelling rule!

a) pop   **b)** set

c) bat   **d)** sip

e) cut   **f)** fix

2 Practise spelling the **-ing** words in activity 1: look, say, cover, write and check each word **three** times.

3 These words have the endings **-ed**, **-ing**, **-er**, **-est** or **-y**, but they have not been spelled correctly. Write out the correct spellings.

a) sun ➜ suny

b) pat ➜ pated

c) mad ➜ mader

d) trip ➜ triping

e) dim ➜ dimest

4 Complete the sentences by adding the correct endings to the words in brackets so they make sense.

a) The fastest (run) _____ won the race.

b) My big sister was the (fit) _____ of all the footballers on her team.

c) The singers were (hum) _____ the tune.

d) My brother's boots were really (mud) _____ .

e) We watched as the player (bat) _____ the ball.

How did you do?

Adding suffixes 2

If a word ends with a consonant plus **e**, you drop the **e** before adding the suffixes **-ed**, **-ing**, **-er**, **-est** or **-y**.

Examples:

hik**e** → hik**ed**, hik**ing**, hik**er**

danc**e** → danc**ed**, danc**ing**, danc**er**

charg**e** → charg**ed**, charg**ing**, charg**er**

bak**e** → bak**ed**, bak**ing**, bak**er**

nic**e** → nic**er**, nic**est**

nos**e** → nos**y**

 Warm up

1 Add **-ing** to these words. Remember the spelling rule!

a) love

b) care

c) race

d) write

e) glare

2 Practise spelling the words in activity 1: look, say, cover, write and check each word **three** times.

3 The words in **bold** will help you find the answers to these clues. Write out the answers.

a) A person who rides a **bike**.

b) A person who goes **hiking**.

c) An adjective for something covered in **slime**.

d) An adjective for food that has lots of **spices**.

Challenge yourself

4 Write out the words in brackets with the correct suffix.

a) My gran's hair is very (wave) _____ .

b) Fred's puppy is cute, and so is Habib's – but mine is the (cute) _____ .

c) I polished the glass until it was very (shine) _____ .

d) Last year, Dad (save) _____ some money for our holiday.

e) It is (safe) _____ to cross a road at a zebra crossing than in other places.

How did you do?

Adding suffixes 3

If a word ends with a consonant plus **y**, change the **y** to **i** before adding the suffixes **-ed**, **-er** or **-est**.

But when adding the suffix **-ing**, keep the **y**!

Examples:

copy ➜ cop**i**er, cop**i**ed, cop**y**ing

happy ➜ happ**i**er, happ**i**est

cry ➜ cr**i**ed, cr**y**ing

Warm up

1 Add the suffixes **-ed** and **-ing** to these words.

a) fry

b) try

c) spy

d) carry

e) hurry

2 Practise spelling the words in activity 1: look, say, cover, write and check each word **three** times.

Answers

Pages 4–5
1. **b)** knee
   c) knock
   d) knuckle
3. **a)** knife
   b) gnaw
   c) knitting
   d) gnash
5. knight, knot(s), knight, knee

Pages 6–7
1. **a)** wrong
   b) wrote
   c) wriggle
   d) wrapper
   e) wrestle
   f) wrap
   g) wrinkle
   h) wren
2. **a)** wrist
   b) wrap
   c) wrote
3. **a)** wreck
   b) correct
   c) written
   d) wrinkle
   e) correct

Pages 8–9
1. **a)** ankle
   b) juggle
   c) needle
   d) puddle
   e) muddle
   f) fiddle
   g) huddle
   h) struggle
3. **a)** middle
   b) cuddle
   c) riddle
   d) paddle
4. **a)** table
   b) candle
   c) bottle
   d) apple

Pages 10–11
1. **a)** hospital
   b) parcel
   c) petal
   d) gerbil
3. **a)** pupil
   b) nostril

c) animal
d) metal
e) petal
5. camel, tunnel, gerbil, kennel, cereal, squirrel, crystal

Pages 12–13
1. **a)** ladies
   b) countries
   c) bodies
   d) stories

3. **Ending in a consonant plus y**:
   copy, copies;
   party, parties;
   diary, diaries;
   city, cities.
   Ending in a vowel plus y:
   key, keys;
   toy, toys;
   journey, journeys;
   day, days.
4. **a)** hurries, plays
   b) tries, says
   c) lays, carries

Pages 14–15
1. **b)** farmyard
   c) dishwasher
   d) toothbrush
   e) footprint
   f) haircut
2. **The compound words are:**
   a) butterfly
   c) eyebrow
   d) fireplace
   f) downstairs
3. **Answers will vary, but make sure the answer given is a real word.**
   Some examples:
   a) homemade, homesick, homework
   b) playground, playhouse, playroom
   c) headache, headlight, headline, headmistress, headphones, headstand
   d) rainbow, raincoat, rainfall, rainforest
   e) snowball, snowboard, snowflake, snowman, snowmobile, snowshoe, snowstorm
   Words that are not compounds include: homeless, homely; player, playful; heads, heady; raining, rainy; snowing, snowy.

Answers

Pages 16–17
1. knight
2. knocked
3. knuckles
4. wrapped
5. wrote
6. Gnashing
7. title
8. muddle
9. little
10. journeys
11. countries
12. stories
13. boys
14. petal
15. camel
16. pencil
17. lighthouse
18. seaside
19. underpants
20. dustbin

Pages 18–19
1. a) popping
   b) setting
   c) batting
   d) sipping
   e) cutting
   f) fixing
3. a) sunny
   b) patted
   c) madder
   d) tripping
   e) dimmest
4. a) runner
   b) fittest
   c) humming
   d) muddy
   e) batted

Pages 20–21
1. a) loving
   b) caring
   c) racing
   d) writing
   e) glaring
3. a) biker
   b) hiker
   c) slimy
   d) spicy
4. a) wavy
   b) cutest
   c) shiny

   d) saved
   e) safer

Pages 22–23
1. a) fried, frying
   b) tried, trying
   c) spied, spying
   d) carried, carrying
   e) hurried, hurrying
3. a) tried
   b) happier
   c) replying
   d) copied
4. a) happiest, married
   b) replied, hurried
   c) heavier, heaviest
   d) lazier

Pages 24–25
1. a) hear
   b) here
   c) sea
   d) see
   e) there
   f) their
2. a) sun
   b) blew
   c) night
   d) bear
3. The homophones are used correctly in b and c.

Pages 26–27
1. a) teacher's
   b) friend's
   c) Dad's
   d) horse's
   e) driver's
   f) Jemaal's
2. a) the dog's tail
   b) Sid's gloves
   c) my grandmother's flowers
   d) Chiyoko's ring
3. a) Erin's
   b) teacher's
   c) goalkeeper's
   d) Mrs Bond's

Pages 28–29
1. have not – haven't
   we have – we've
   they will – they'll
   it is – it's
2. a) they're
   b) you've

c) couldn't
d) he's
e) I'll
f) didn't
3. a) don't
b) doesn't
c) he'd
d) We've

Pages 30–31
1. Olivia's
2. cousin's
3. car's
4. uncle's
5. too/two
6. bee
7. toe
8. so/sow (as in sowing seeds)
9. didn't
10. I've
11. couldn't
12. carried
13. hurried
14. cried
15. berries
16. keys
17. shaker
18. copier
19. hummed, humming
20. tipped, tipping

Pages 32–33
1. a) payment
b) statement
c) astonishment
d) excitement
3. a) darkness
b) softness
c) weakness
d) tiredness
4. a) replacement
b) equipment
c) sadness
d) pavement
e) measurement
f) crispiness
g) punishment
h) cheekiness

Pages 34–35
1. a) cheerful
b) tearful
c) delightful

d) dreadful
e) peaceful
2. a) harmless
b) tasteless
c) voiceless
d) homeless
3. a) penniless
b) careful, careless
c) hurtful
d) beautiful
e) breathless

Pages 36–37
1. a) question
b) education
c) exclamation
d) explanation
e) information
3. a) addition
b) subtraction
c) description
d) action
4. a) section
b) position
c) invitation
d) lotion
e) station

Pages 38–39
1. a) madly
b) quickly
c) slowly
d) quietly
e) famously
2. a) angrily
b) hungrily
c) happily
d) busily
e) funnily
4. a) carefully
b) noisily
c) bravely
d) brightly
e) calmly
Sentences will vary, but they should contain these adverbs used correctly in context.

Pages 40–41
1. a) ledge
b) ridge
c) sledge
d) barge

e) charge
f) cage
g) edge

2.

b	a	d	g	e	r		
	g						
h	e	d	g	e	h	o	g
e			o		u		
d			r	a	g	e	
g			g		e		
e			e				

3. a) stage
    b) badge
    c) hedge
    d) large

Pages 42–43
1. calmly
2. nearly
3. noisily
4. nosily
5. prettily
6. nation
7. station
8. invitation
9. mention
10. condition
11. sadness
12. entertainment
13. pointless
14. beautiful
15. ledge
16. hedge
17. fudge
18. bridge
19. charge
20. cage

3 Choose the correct word in **bold** to complete each sentence.

a) I **tryed / tried** very hard to learn my times tables.

b) We felt much **happyer / happier** once we had met our new teacher.

c) Just as I was **replying / repliing** to our teacher's question, the fire bell rang.

d) Sanjay **copyed / copied** his spellings neatly into his book.

Challenge yourself

4 Add the suffixes **-ed**, **-er** or **-est** to the words in brackets and write them out.

a) My uncle was the (happy) _____ he had ever been when he (marry) _____ Sarah.

b) Today, we (reply) _____ to our cousin's invitation and we (hurry) _____ to buy her a present.

c) I am (heavy) _____ than my sister, but my brother is the (heavy) _____ .

d) Our cat is lazy, but our dog is even (lazy) _____ .

How did you do?

Homophones

Words that sound the same but have a different spelling and meaning are called **homophones**.

> **Examples:**
>
> | | | |
> |---|---|---|
> | here | hear | |
> | see | sea | |
> | bare | bear | |
> | to | too | two |
> | there | their | they're |

Warm up

1. Choose the correct homophone to complete each sentence, and write it out.

   a) I _____ with my ears.   **here / hear**

   b) Come over _____.   **here / hear**

   c) Look at the waves in the _____.   **see / sea**

   d) I _____ with my eyes.   **see / sea**

   e) My brother's over _____.   **their / there**

   f) They were walking _____ dog.   **their / there**

2 Choose the correct word from the box to complete each sentence, and write it out.

| blew | blue | bear | bare | night | knight | sun | son |

a) It was really hot in the _____ today.

b) The wild wind _____ all night long.

c) You can see the moon and the stars at _____ .

d) The brown _____ climbed up the tree.

Challenge yourself

3 In **two** of the sentences below, the pairs of homophones are used incorrectly. Can you identify in which **two** sentences they are used correctly?

a) There very helpful to they're teacher.

b) I won two prizes at the fair but I lost one.

c) When I knew it was my baby brother's birthday, I bought him a new toy.

d) It is to cold too go outside today.

How did you do?

Apostrophes to show possession

You can show that something **belongs** to someone by using an **apostrophe** and the letter **s**. The apostrophe goes between the last letter of the word and the letter **s**.

> **Examples:**
>
> Abeba**'s** scarf is pretty. (The scarf belongs to Abeba.)
>
> My brother**'s** football has burst. (The football belongs to my brother.)

 Warm up

1 Decide where to insert an apostrophe in each of the words in **bold**, and write out the correct word.

a) Our **teachers** computer has been mended.

b) My **friends** coat is the same as mine.

c) **Dads** favourite food is fruit.

d) The **horses** stable was warm and cosy.

e) The **drivers** eyes were getting tired so she stopped for a break.

f) **Jemaals** tennis game was cancelled.

2 Write out these phrases so that they use an apostrophe to show that something belongs to someone. An example has been done for you.

> **Example:**
>
> the book belonging to Sami ➔ *Sami's book*

a) the tail belonging to the dog

b) the gloves belonging to Sid

c) the flowers belonging to my grandmother

d) the ring belonging to Chiyoko

Challenge yourself

3 Pick the most suitable person to fit into each sentence, then write the person down with an apostrophe in the right place.

goalkeeper	Mrs Bond	Erin	teacher

a) My friend _____ hat was under your desk.

b) My _____ handwriting is very neat.

c) We all cheered the _____ save.

d) _____ broken leg has mended.

How did you do?

Apostrophes to make words shorter

You can sometimes make two words into one shorter word by taking away a letter or letters. You need to put the **apostrophe** just above where the **missing letters** would be.

> **Examples:**
>
> **I am** hot. → **I'm** hot.
>
> **You are** seven years old. → **You're** seven years old.
>
> **The cat is** purring. → The **cat's** purring.

Warm up

1 Match the words in Column A with their shortened form in Column B, and write them out together.

Column A	Column B
have not	it's
we have	haven't
they will	they'll
it is	we've

2 Use an apostrophe to turn each pair of words into one word, and write out the words.

a) they are

b) you have

c) could not

d) he is

e) I will

f) did not

Challenge yourself

3 The apostrophes have been put in the wrong place in each of the words in **bold** in these sentences. Write out the words correctly.

a) We **dont'** understand!

b) Milo **does'nt** want to play.

c) Grandad said **hed'** show me how to do it.

d) **Wev'e** finished our toast.

4 Practise spelling the words in activity 3: look, say, cover, write and check each word **three** times.

How did you do?

Progress test 2

For each word in **bold**, decide where to put an apostrophe to show possession, then write the word down with the apostrophe in the correct place.

1 **Olivias** new table tennis bat is expensive.

2 My **cousins** school report wasn't very good.

3 That **cars** headlight isn't working.

4 Our **uncles** house is enormous.

Write a homophone for each of the following words:

5 to

6 be

7 tow

8 sew

Using an apostrophe, write the shortened form of these words:

9 did not

10 I have

11 could not

Add **-ed** to the following verbs ending in **y**. Remember the spelling rule!

12 carry

13 hurry

14 cry

Write down the plural form of the following nouns ending in **y**. Remember the spelling rule!

15 one berry   lots of...

16 my key   our...

Add **-er** to these words. Remember the spelling rule!

17 shake

18 copy

Add **-ed** and **-ing** to these words. Remember the spelling rule!

19 hum

20 tip

Making nouns with suffixes

You can add the **suffixes -ness** and **-ment** to most **root words** to make a noun, without changing the last letter of the word you started with.

> **Examples:**
>
> enjoy → enjoy**ment**
>
> sad → sad**ness**

But there are some exceptions; in some words of more than one syllable ending in a consonant + **y**, the **y** is changed to **i**.

> **Examples:**
>
> happy → happ**i**ness
>
> floppy → flopp**i**ness

Warm up

1 Add the suffix **-ment** to the following words.

a) pay

b) state

c) astonish

d) excite

2 Practise spelling the words in activity 1: look, say, cover, write and check each word **three** times.

3 Add the suffix **-ness** to each word in brackets, then write it out.

a) We headed into the (dark) _____ of the night.

b) I love the (soft) _____ of my baby brother's hair.

c) After my fall, I was left with a (weak) _____ in my legs.

d) My (tired) _____ lasted all day.

Challenge yourself

4 Decide whether each word takes **-ment** or **-ness** to turn it into a noun. Watch out for words ending in **y**! Write out the words.

a) replace

b) equip

c) sad

d) pave

e) measure

f) crispy

g) punish

h) cheeky

How did you do?

Making adjectives with suffixes

You can add the suffixes **-ful** or **-less** to some nouns to make an adjective, without changing the last letter of the root word.

When we add the suffix **-ful**, the adjective usually has a positive meaning. When we add the suffix **-less**, the meaning becomes negative.

> **Examples:**
>
> care → care**ful**, care**less**
>
> hope → hope**ful**, hope**less**

But there is an exception to this rule; in words of more than one syllable ending in a consonant plus **y**, the **y** is changed to **i**.

> **Examples:**
>
> beaut**y** → beaut**iful**
>
> penn**y** → penn**iless**

Warm up

1 Add the suffix **-ful** to the following words and write them down.

a) cheer

b) tear

c) delight

d) dread

e) peace

2 Add the suffix **-less** to each word in brackets and write it down.

a) The berries looked (harm) _____ but we decided not to touch them anyway.

b) We tried to eat the (taste) _____ pie but it was simply too awful.

c) My auntie's bad cold has left her (voice) _____.

d) After the floods, many people were (home) _____.

3 Decide whether each word takes **-ful**, **-less** or **both** to turn it into an adjective. Watch out for words ending in **y**! Write the words out.

a) penny

b) care

c) hurt

d) beauty

e) breath

Words ending in -tion

The suffix **-tion** appears at the end of lots of English root words. It is pronounced **shun**.

Examples:

celebra**tion**

condi**tion**

fic**tion**

mo**tion**

 Warm up

1️⃣ Add the suffix **-tion** to each of these word beginnings.

a) ques _____

b) educa _____

c) exclama _____

d) explana _____

e) informa _____

2️⃣ Practise spelling the words in activity 1: look, say, cover, write and check each word **three** times.

3 These words all end in **-tion** but their letters have been jumbled up. Unravel them and write the correct spelling.

a) addinoti

b) ontisubtrac

c) descripniot

d) actino

$$4(4x)+2(x) = 72$$
$$x = ?$$

Challenge yourself

4 The words in **bold** in these sentences have been spelled incorrectly. Write out the correct spelling for each.

a) Our teacher read a small **secshun** of the text.

b) It is important to place an apostrophe in the correct **posishun**.

c) My friend Stan sent me an **invitashun** to his party.

d) Grandma used her favourite body **loshun** to keep her hands soft.

e) Mum dropped Jenna off at the bus **stashun**.

How did you do?

Making adverbs with the suffix -ly

Adverbs can give you more **information** about the **verb** (doing or being word) in a sentence. Many **adverbs** end in the suffix **-ly**. For most words, you just add **-ly** to the root word.

Examples:

bad ➜ bad**ly**

sad ➜ sad**ly**

But if the root word ends in a consonant plus **y** and has **more than one syllable**, then you need to change the **y** to **i** before adding **-ly**.

Example:

happ**y** ➜ happ**i**ly

Warm up

1 Add the suffix **-ly** to each of these adjectives to make an adverb.

a) mad_____

b) quick_____

c) slow_____

d) quiet_____

e) famous_____

2 Add **-ly** to each of these words. Remember the spelling rule: for adjectives with more than one syllable ending in a **consonant** plus **y**, you need to change the **y** to **i**.

a) angry

b) hungry

c) happy

d) busy

e) funny

3 Practise writing the adverbs from activity 2 **three** times.

4 Turn these adjectives into adverbs, then write a sentence containing each one.

a) careful

b) noisy

c) brave

d) bright

e) calm

How did you do?

Words spelled with *dge* and *ge*

Apart from at the beginning of words, as in jam or jump, the letter **j** is hardly ever used to make the **j** sound. Instead, when the **j** sound follows a short vowel sound, it is spelled **dge**; and when the **j** sound follows a long vowel sound or a consonant, it is spelled **ge**.

Examples:

bri**dge** (short vowel sound)

hu**ge** (long vowel sound)

Warm up

1 Add either **-dge** or **-ge** to make a word that makes sense. Say each word out loud to hear the vowel sound before you write it.

a) le_____

b) ri_____

c) sle_____

d) bar_____

e) char_____

f) ca_____

g) e_____

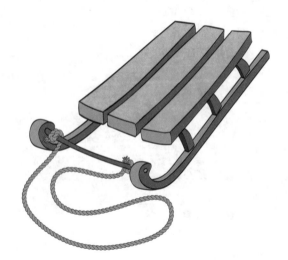

2 The letters **ge** and **dge** are missing from the words in this grid. Write each word out in full.

b	a				r		
h					h	o	g
e			o		u		
			r	a			

Challenge yourself

3 Write down the missing words from the sentences that end in either **-dge** or **-ge**.

a) My cousin sings on the sta_____ .

b) I was given a special ba_____ to wear for my birthday.

c) Zara kicked the ball over the he_____ .

d) A lar_____ bee flew in through the window.

How did you do?

Turn these adjectives into adverbs by adding the suffix **-ly**.

1 calm

2 near

3 noisy

4 nosy

5 pretty

The endings of these words have been written as they sound. Rewrite them correctly.

6 nashun

7 stashun

8 invitashun

9 menshun

10 condishun

Add **-less**, **-ful**, **-ness** or **-ment** to each of the following words.

11 sad

12 entertain

13 point

14 beauty

These words have been spelled as they sound. Write them out, using the correct ending, either **-ge** or **-dge**.

15 lej

16 hej

17 fuj

18 brij

19 charj

20 caje

Published by Keen Kite Books
An imprint of HarperCollins*Publishers* Ltd
The News Building
1 London Bridge Street
London SE1 9GF

ISBN 9780008184544

First published in 2016

10 9 8 7 6 5 4 3 2 1

Series Concept and Commissioning: Michelle I'Anson
Series Editor and Development: Shelley Teasdale & Fiona Watson
Inside Concept Design: Paul Oates
Project Manager: Rebecca Adlard
Cover Design: Anthony Godber
Text Design and Layout: Q2A Media
Production: Lyndsey Rogers
Printed in the UK

A CIP record of this book is available from the British Library.

Images are ©Shutterstock.com